FeNiX RiZiN. A poetic journey throughout my years of finding myself through raising others to their fullest potential

Trelena Hamner

BookLeaf Publishing

India | USA | UK

Presentation by *BookLeaf Publishing*

Web: www.bookleafpub.com

E-mail: info@bookleafpub.com

ISBN: 9789360943509

First edition 2024

I dedicate this book to my Dad. Even though he is not with me anymore in this physical world, he is with me every day in everything I do. I love you Dad and I miss you every moment

ACKNOWLEDGEMENT

I want to acknowledge my biggest fans. First My Mother, Lora Banks, she had faith in me when I couldn't understand the word.
My first born Son, my SUN, Daniel Robertson, who motivated me to keep writing even when I didn't want to pick up a pen. And to my PAL, Joshua Dennison, who has shown me that love does not have to hurt and has given me support in my current journey to find my dreams
Thank you all so much for just being who you are

The Hippie Way

Short and sweet is how I roll
Twist a joint or smoke a bowl
My eyes are squinty
My mouth is dry
I laugh and giggle
And don't know why
I love to LAUGH
I love to PLAY
And that's my LIFE
THE HIPPIE WAY

Mirror Image

Mirror Mirror on the wall
I'm not thin
I'm not small
Beauty, Kindness
And intelligent
Is what I see
Shapely and Short
It's all Me
Accept the image
Below and above
God made Me perfect
With His everlasting
LOVE

Mommie

A long distance hug
An over the phone smile
May carry us thru
For a little while

Our bond is solid
Like no other in the world
An amazing Mommie
With her Baby girl

Many different words
Fall in me like rain
Yet trying to describe the feeling
Overloads my brain

I want to say so much
But whee to start
The "Word Nerd"
Can't describe
The feelings of her Heart

For days now I have worried
How do I say
What can I do

The truest way
To simply say

I LOVE YOU
Always,
Your Baby Girl

I wrote this from my mother obviously, and I
really can't remember why. But I struggled with
trying to describe how I feel for her, my own
mother! I wasn't always so nice to her while I
was growing up, it took distance, growth, and
becoming a mother myself, to realize what I
owed her. After all I had put her through I owed
her the best daughter mother and human I could
be. I will strive to make her proud of me
everyday. All the embarrassment I caused her
over time, the only thing I could do to correct
some of my actions was to be my best. To show
her how great of a parent she was and is. I can
only be the "Baby Girl" she raised.
Lessons learned mom. And like all the other
things I had to learn to do it myself.
    Trelena Hamner

The Way Men Lie

5

The way men lie I think ADAM bit the Apple
first and blamed it on Eve.
She was so deviantly devoted and loyal
she accepted the ACCUSATIONS
Shielding her HUSBAND
 From all the arrows
     Of
JUDGEMENT
RIDICULE
    and
HATRED
Forever throughout
  TIME

Lil Man

An angel standing at your feet.
Waiting patiently to sit and eat.
Colored cereal with sugar all over.
Rainbow stars and lucky clovers.

Slowly and perfectly tying his shoe.
Twisting around in his chair
Not to miss any of blue's clues.

Bundled up in his coat
backpack in hand.
Your silently crying
Looking down at your little man.

Watching him grow all the way
 to his senior year.
"I'm joining the army"
 is the last thing you want to hear.

No more will he ask you,
"mommy can I hold your hand?"
All grown up until a young man.

he's on his way out now
To start his own life.

Making a future for himself.
Finding himself a future wife.

As he speaks his vows
standing proud and tall.
Professing his love in front of us all

Memories come rushing in
with tears you didn't plan.
Cuz even now
 when he's looking down

He's still your little man

Cookie cutter Jaws

8

Exalt your difference
Embrace your Flaws

Protect who YOU ARE
 from
COOKIE CUTTER JAWS

Pencil N Pen

9

As I sit down to doodle
I can't help but think

Do I keep drawing in pencil
Or write my rhymes in ink.

My imagination overpowers me
So much I overflow.
Creativity uncontrollable
Just go go.

Pictures through my pencil.
Words through my pen.

Always the beginning
But never an end.

As my adventures change
My mind will expand.

I have most definitely
Learned pencil and pen
Go hand in hand.

Faithful Copilot

Hope N love
  Solid N strong
Not for the short haul
  down for the long.

Adventures at every turn
  mile after mile.
I would travel the universe
  just to see you smile.

Our connection is permanent
  like tractor and trailer
Put together on earth
  by heavenly factor.

driver and co-pilot
  our Savior rides along
Traveling through life with
  Hope N love

Solid N strong

Explaining Recovery

Recovery is like an ocean,
And the addict is adrift on a
        raft.
I mean alone,no land in sight;no help in the
distance.
        nothing.
Except a hole in your body taken up by shakes
you can't
        stop.
Taking up by nightmares,only called such
because you
        enjoy them.

 You see addiction is his voice in your head a
voice all the way in the back that says, "It's okay
to be NUMB, "It's okay to SUCCUMB to your
urge to LEAVE REALITY behind",because it
has no place for you"

 That voice is so sweet, sometimes that you may
lean in to listen, until your RAFT SHIFTS

It's a SIREN song LURING you to a grave

caught up in the NUMBNESS and
DEPRESSION.

 The ocean never ends it doesn't matter how far
you go, or who will find you along the way.

 it's like you're CONNECTED, but the message
   NEVER SENDS.
 that's why I don't try to EXPLAIN recovery to
my "NON-ADDICT" friends.

Written BY MY SON
DANIELL ROBERTSON

THIS WAS WRITTEN BY MY SON WHEN I
WAS IN FULL ADDICTION AND
ADDICTED TO INTRAVENOUS
METHAMPHETAMINE MY HUSBAND AT
THE TIME WAS ALSO VERY ADDICTED
AND WE WERE ON A ROAD OF DISASTER
A ROAD TO OUR GRAVES AND THIS IS
HOW MY SON TRIED TO EXPLAIN
RECOVERY TO ME AND HOW IT FELT.
BEING AN ADDICT. BECAUSE HE
HIMSELF HAD BEEN AN ADDICT AS
WELL AND WAS IN RECOVERY AND IS
STILL CURRENTLY IN RECOVERY. SO I
FOUND IT FITTING BECAUSE HE IS MY

S.O.N. AND MY S.U.N. THAT THIS BE IN
THIS COMPILATION

Hiding Me

To the woman who raised me
how could you
how could you
how could you be

so beautiful and caring
so loving to me
from crawling to walking
from dating and tears

standing by me
Mending My broken heart
chasing away my fears.

Nightmares and screams
Goals to dreams
when I felt my lowes
you were always picking me up it seems

After all the arguments n the fights
how could you be
Strong,patient,protective
loving
Always seeing
the hiding me

Just Simple Thoughts

1. Uniqueness: The ZEN level of
AWESOMENESS

2. COOKIE CUTTER SOCIETY
    Only leaves STALE CRUMBS
    On a STYROFOAM PLATE

3. BE HUMBLE AND KIND TO SOCIETY
    ON A GROUND LEVEL
    Only REAL and TRUE Souls out in the time
    into climbing UP in the UNIVERSE
    to understand how to stay
    HUMBLE AND KIND

4. FLOWERS are NATURES way of bringing
    the SMALLEST PIECE OF IF BEAUTY
    to the FEW that TAKES THE TIME
    TO NOTICE

5. THE MELODY IF YOUR SOUL
    RADIATES THRU THE
    SINGING IG YOUR CHARACTER

6. AMONG THE DARKEST, DRYEST, SOLID
    FIELDS IF CRAB GRASS

HIDES THE SMALLEST SEEDS
OF REBIRTH

Creativity Blooms

Creativity first blooms through mixing crayons
to make black.
Locked in the evening cartoons
 with a cup of strawberry milk and a bedtime
snack.

Growing into imaginary Friends
dancing all around
dressing up an old clothes
cardboard rockets that never leave the ground.

Acceptance and nurture bring
creativity waves that
  multiply
      building &
          INCREASE
FLooding our spirits with
    love
      happiness
          equality &
            PEACE

Society PUSHES creativity down
 covers it up
Locks it in the DARK

Imaginary Friends become demons
spiritual dancing quickly
turns into a MARCH

Too file into a forced worldly ROUTINE.
Where happiness is not real &
 love is on the GUILLOTINE .

exalt imperfections they had character
An invaluable RESOURCE

Honestly who wrote the rules
to set what's par for the COURSE.

Thoughts from a 5 yr old

I wrote this about you like event when I was
about 5 years old

I don't understand why daddy isn't coming to
Grandma's with us
I'm so excited to go
But mommy seems sad.

Grandma lives far away
we are moving there Mommy said
But if we're not coming back
what about my dad.

maybe they are just so upset with each other.
or they had a fight.
I hear them argue and sometimes yell
I even heard banging at night
maybe daddy fell.

I am not scared of a new place
or even being with family that I don't really
know
But it's just going to be us three mommy says.
Just me,her and Joe.

Daddy didn't want to come he was going to stay.
I know he will miss us being so far away. my
mommy said we can call him
each and every day.

why don't Daddy answer?
is he not at home?
maybe he is outside working,
he can't hear the phone

he works outside a lot with all his tools
but it's been a while since we talked
I'm fixin to start school.

Mommy says Daddy is coming to visit picking
us up to play.
I was so happy when she told me.
where is he at it's already Sunday?!

I have school tomorrow I can't wait
maybe it's cuz I bragged to my classmates

Teasing about not having a dad hurts my feelings
makes me mad
so I told him he was coming to school for Show
and Tell.
With pride and some tears
and it's because I lied
        that

he
    isn't
        here!

My Dad passed away 3 yrs ago. I never thought
I would have to loose him twice in One Lifetime

Originality

22

Originality creates Somebody's

Conformity creates Everybody's

Doesn't EVERYBODY want to be
SOMEBODY

Lights in your eyes

How do you turn off the lights in your eyes
 With pain sorrow and tragedy & lies
Betrayal to your soul
Down to the core
A continuous open wound
An invisible bleeding sore.

No healing can be done due to the shame
 So you shut down your feelings
Emotions
 Build high walls around you
To keep others from doing the same.

The switch is destroyed never to be turned
 Back on.
Darkness becomes your normal
There is no Dawn.

You're only protected by yourself
 Defense is your lifestyle
Searching every dark corner to find
 Anything that keeps the world away for Awhile.

Uppers downers or combo of both
 Death is welcome

There is no hope.

To find healing that just doesn't exist
 Just stop the fighting.
Give up and quit.

Life goes on and you live OF the world not IN
it.
People are vile and devious
You just can't take the SHIT

Fake smiles on their FACE
False words in their mouths
EVILNESS so deep within them
Honesty Truth Love & Goodness
Have absolutely no SPACE!!

Poison flows from them
Demolishing inner peace
Destruction brings NO SLEEP

Always on the Defensive
Watching around every corner
Concentrating on the Dark

Turning off the LIGHTS IN YOUR EYES
Is the Only Way to see
The Satanic Mark

Alot of Hats

How can I be TWO people at once?
or THREE or FOUR?
I'm running in circles
Just looking for the door

Does the craziness end
Or continue forever?
One voice says yes
But the others YELL NEVER

My mind is so clouded
it just wants it just won't clear
the voices are so loud
it rings in my ears

the dark won't last always
at least that's what I hope
I don't want to spend the rest of my life
depending on dope.

stuck in the darkness with no end in sight
I wake every morning praying for the light

 just one person is all I want to be
I'll wear a lot of hats
but I just want to be me

Hide N Seek

26

Hide and seek is a game we play
Searching for sunlight everyday

looking around this corner
or maybe the other side
the harder we seek it
the deeper it hides

test of strength is the struggle we're in
alone we could lose it
but together we win

hide and seek is a game we play
we WILL find the sunlight
make the darkness go away

Room full of People

In a room full of people
I feel totally alone
can't find my way out
I just want to go home

room is getting smaller
it's harder to breathe.
I finally start to choke
and I hear you cry for me

over all the voices bouncing around in my head
out of the screaming
I can only hear you instead

the lights are out now
I'm stuck in the dark
waiting for you to light a match
longing for the spark

united we stand
divided we fall
our lives are still go on
we've already been through it all

my head will stop spinning

I'll be able to stand
only if you're beside me holding my hand

Tik tok goes the clock

Tick tock goes the clock
as the world spins round N round
tick tock goes the clock in the center of town

 Christmas carolers sing joyfully in the night
The magic of the city
what a powerful sight

its the time of year to show peace and love the
reason for the season comes from above

such an electric time can't be undone
be thankful, rejoice and celebrate
the father and the son

Craved Love

Hatred is heavy
drowning me in fear and sorrow

I have to leave it so I can move to tomorrow

It attacks me and yes so loudly
it clogs my ears
where's the soft voice for my younger years the
soft voice of Jesus
calling My name I heard him and answered now
life will never be the same

I can hear the birds
smell the flowers
I find myself smiling and laughing for hours

My hatred is taken
my soul is saved
I found the belonging and love
that I have craved

God's Crayon Box

This isn't really a poem just a comparison I
thought of during a church service but I still
think you'll like it

God's crayon box

Personalities in God's family is like a big box of
crayons
He is always in search of the missing ones each
and everyone is dear to his heart.
they can't be a replacement.
He keeps looking and searching for his lost
crayons brand new or worn down with the paper
torn & gone.
each one is just as important to the Lord
especially the Broken, Chipped, covered in dirt
from under the couch.
God never stop calling for you.
The day you answer there is joy in heaven cuz
his family is whole again and
His crayon box is full.